D1308214

VINTAGE
Pies

*Classic American Pies
for Today's Home Baker*

Anne Haynie Collins

Photographs by Lisa and Todd Balfour

THE COUNTRYMAN PRESS
WOODSTOCK, VERMONT

Photographs © Balfour Studios
Book design and composition by Eugenie S. Delaney

Published by The Countryman Press, P.O. Box 748,
Woodstock, VT 05091
Distributed by W. W. Norton & Company, Inc., 500 Fifth Avenue,
New York, NY 10110
Printed in the United States of America

Library of Congress Cataloging-in-Publication Data are available

Vintage Pies
978-1-58157-264-3

10 9 8 7 6 5 4 3 2 1

Contents

Chapter 3—Cake Pies

Chapter 4—Custard Pies

Acknowledgments

I'd like to thank the people who made this idea a reality: my sister, Cynthia, for seeing a book in my recipe cards; Michele, for thinking I could do this; John, Mojgan, Daniel, and Michael, for being my Dallas pie tasters, and Beth, Lucia, and Susan, for being my Houston pie tasters; Drea, for honestly critiquing nearly a dozen blueberry pies; the good people of Bill Beck Real Estate in Middlebury, Vermont—Tom, Jan, Jackie, Peter, Debbie, Judy, Ray, and Erin—for diligently tasting every single pie in this book; Pat and Tom for their help in creating the photos that piqued a publisher's interest; B.K., Phyllis, Margaret, Dana, Shari, Barbara, Jim, and Anne, for their enthusiasm and support; and the best photographers ever, Lisa and Todd Balfour. I would also like to remember my sister Hilary and my friend Coleen; neither lived to see this book completed, but both helped to make it happen.

And this section wouldn't be complete without thanking my son, Andy, who, even though not a sweet-eater, good-naturedly tried everything; Thomas-the-bad-dog, for keeping the floor clean; and my partner and companion, my husband, Brian. You make the journey worthwhile.

Introduction

"No pie-eating people can be permanently vanquished."

—*New York Times*, 1902

*P*ies were once a staple of the American table. My grandmother, Pearl Thomas, was born Pearl Savage in 1894, and she remembered her grandmother, Nancy Stone, baking up to a dozen pies each week, to feed her family and the farmhands. Pies were baked fresh in the morning and served at noon, with the day's main meal; a slice of pie, wrapped in a cloth napkin, went in a tin pail to the fields for midafternoon. Pie was served cold, with a glass of buttermilk, at supper, and again for breakfast. Pies graced Sunday dinner tables, quilting bees, and wedding suppers, and fed grieving families.

I became fascinated with old pie recipes as a child, and have been collecting them for over 40 years—heirloom pies, I suppose we would call them today, as they come from a time before the advent of such ingredients as corn syrup and artificial food colorings. My primary sources were elderly people, and my method was simple: asking them to tell me their favorite pie from childhood, and about pies that weren't made any longer. If someone didn't have a recipe for me, I'd thumb through old cookbooks until I found one, or, failing that, I'd reengineer a modern recipe with traditional ingredients. Then I'd bake it up and have them test it. Food-memory is an amazing thing, and my victims would let me know immediately if the taste and consistency were right. (Or, probably more importantly, if not.) What I did not realize, until I began the research for this book, was how old these recipes actually were, with many of them dating to the earliest days of this country.

The recipe for piecrust comes from Nancy Stone. It's a good crust, flaky, but sturdy enough to stand up to any filling. The fillings are simple, but delicious, and make use of the ingredients that a farm- or housewife would have had on hand in her larder. And these recipes speak to the ingenuity and thrift of those women, using sometimes improbable ingredients, and letting nothing go to waste.

Pies are not meant to be food art. (Although, on a good day, they can be.) Pie-crusts shrink or have to be patched, fillings bubble over, meringues weep. But a pie's purpose is not to be beautiful; rather, to be eaten and savored.

A Few Notes

All of the recipes make 9-inch pies. When I first began baking, an 8-inch-diameter pie plate was considered the standard size; today 9-inch is the standard, and 8-inch pie plates have almost disappeared. (One slice of 9-inch pie will have 26 percent more calories than a slice of 8-inch pie.)

In this book, every pie bakes at 350°F. Until fairly recently, bakers didn't have the luxury of variable-temperature ovens—the temperature you had was the temperature you had. An advantage to a single baking temperature is that you can bake any of the pies together.

In the days before refrigeration, butter was salted to retard spoilage. So in the recipes that call for butter, I've used lightly salted rather than unsalted. Please note that in this book, a stick of commercially sold butter is assumed to weigh 4 ounces; if using local or artisan butter, take care to measure out the weight specified in the recipe, as stick sizes may differ.

For recipes using whole milk, I prefer unhomogenized, or cream-on-top, milk. That's the more traditional ingredient, but homogenized milk will work just as well.

If you have access to eggs from free-range chickens, I recommend using them, particularly for pies with lighter-colored fillings. The eggs from free-range chickens usually have bright yellow or orange yolks and make spectacularly beautiful custards.

And, finally, while the recipes in this book will provide you with instructions for doing things the old way, such as boiling your own cider, or steaming your own pumpkin, you will find them equally adaptable to modern life and modern sched-ules. But sometimes it's fun to take a step back in time, and remember how it was once done.

CHAPTER ONE

Piecrust

*This recipe for piecrust has been in
my family since the 1860s. It is
basic, easy to work with,
and very forgiving,
and produces
a light and
flaky
crust.*

Single Piecrust

This will make one generous 9-inch piecrust.

 1 cup unbleached all-purpose flour, plus about ½ cup for kneading and rolling dough
 ½ teaspoon salt
 7 tablespoons lard or solid vegetable shortening
 ¼ cup cold water

If your recipe calls for a prebaked or partially baked crust, preheat your oven to 350°F.

Combine the 1 cup of the flour and the salt in a large bowl with a fork. Put each tablespoon of the lard in a different place on top of the flour mixture. With a pastry blender or two knives, very lightly and quickly cut the lard into the flour mixture to form crumbs about the size of peas.

Sprinkle the cold water over the top of the flour mixture. Stir the mixture with a fork until it just holds together.

Sprinkle a flat work surface with about ¼ cup of flour. Turn the dough out of the bowl onto the floured surface. With your fingertips, lightly and quickly knead the dough just until it's smooth, about 15 strokes.

Gather the dough together with your hands and form it into a ball. Flatten the ball into a thick circle.

I don't chill my pie dough; I just put it directly in the pie plate. Here's why: I learned pie making from my grandmother when I was 10 or 11 (and she was in her mid-70s) and that's the way she did it. It wasn't until much later that I learned that most recipes call for chilling dough.

MAKING PIECRUST

TOP LEFT: **placing lard on flour**

TOP RIGHT: **proper size crumb after cutting in lard**

BOTTOM LEFT: **"coming together" after adding water**

BOTTOM RIGHT: **what kneaded pie dough looks like**

To roll out the dough, sprinkle the flat work surface with more flour. Place your dough on the floured surface, then turn it over so that both sides are floured. Roll out the dough with your rolling pin from the center to the edge with light, even strokes. Occasionally lift the dough so it doesn't stick to the work surface. The shape should be about 1 inch larger on all sides than the pie plate you are using and it should be ⅛ to ¼ inch thick.

Fold the dough in half, and lift it into the pie plate. Unfold the dough, and ease it gently into the pie plate, taking care not to stretch the dough. (Stretching the dough will make the pastry shrink as it bakes, and you'll end up with a piecrust the size of a salad plate. Trust me, I speak from experience.) Press the dough onto the rim of the pie plate, and trim any overhanging bits.

ABOVE: **rolling out the dough**

TOP RIGHT: **rolled out dough**

BOTTOM LEFT: **measuring for the pie plate**

BOTTOM RIGHT: **placing crust in pie plate**

If my piecrust tears while I'm putting it in the pie plate, I'll slightly overlap the torn edges and press the tear with my fingertips to make a good seal.

For a prebaked crust, place the pie plate in the oven, and bake the crust for 15 to 20 minutes; for a partially baked crust, bake it for 7 to 10 minutes. If the bottom begins to bubble up, prick it with a fork. You can also prevent the crust from bubbling up by spreading dried beans or pie weights on it before putting it in the oven. Let it cool completely before you add the filling.

ABOVE LEFT: **trimming the crust with Nancy Stone's pastry trimmer**

ABOVE RIGHT: **crust in pie plate**

RIGHT: **prebaked crust using beans to keep crust flat in pie plate**

Double Piecrust

For a double-crust pie, simply double the recipe. Divide the dough in half, and roll out half of it, as above, for the bottom crust. Roll out the second half for the upper crust. You may use it as a solid crust, or cut it into ¾-inch strips with a pastry cutter or a sharp, floured knife, and weave it into a lattice top.

Note: If you've made three piecrusts, you'll probably have enough dough scraps left over to make a fourth one. Just combine the scraps into a ball, knead it a few times, and then roll it out, as described above. It might be a bit tougher than the first three, but I don't think anyone eating the pie is going to complain too much.

OPPOSITE PAGE
MAKING A SOLID TOP CRUST

TOP LEFT: **folding & lifting**

TOP RIGHT: **cutting vents**

BOTTOM RIGHT: **crimping & sealing**

MAKING A LATTICE TOP CRUST

OPPOSITE TOP: **cutting in strips**

OPPOSITE BOTTOM: **weaving strips**

ABOVE: **ready to go in the oven**

CHAPTER TWO

Transparent Pies

Transparent pies made their appearance
in American cooking as early as the 18th
century, and probably had their origin
in the traditional English Banbury, or
chess, tarts. The basic filling was sugar,
eggs, and butter; the addition of a small
amount of flour or cornmeal created our
American chess pie. Embellishments
would include fruits, nutmeats, spices,
and, occasionally, milk or cream.

Transparent Pie

This old recipe, which dates from the 1700s, makes the simplest of the transparent pies.

1	unbaked piecrust
3	large eggs
1⅛	cups granulated sugar
⅓	cup salted butter

Preheat your oven to 350°F.

In a medium bowl, whisk the eggs until they are light in color. Add the sugar and the butter, and whisk the ingredients until they are well combined. Pour the filling into the piecrust.

Place the pie in the oven, and bake it until the filling is set in the middle, about 35 minutes.

Sugar Pie

A version of transparent pie developed using cane syrup. It was called sugar pie, and, with the addition of pecans, would become pecan pie.

1 unbaked piecrust
⅓ cup salted butter
3 large eggs
1 cup cane syrup or dark corn syrup
⅔ cup granulated sugar

Preheat your oven to 350°F.

In a small saucepan, melt the butter. In a medium bowl, whisk the eggs until they are light. Add the syrup, the sugar, and the butter, and whisk the ingredients until they are well combined. Pour the filling into the piecrust.

Place the pie in the oven, and bake it until the filling is set in the middle, about 40 minutes.

Amber Pie

This is the pie that started it all. When I was little, my mother's family had Decoration Day picnics; at one of them, when I was eight or nine, one of my grandmother's uncles said he "wisht" he had a piece of Pearl's amber pie. I had never heard of amber pie and, when I asked her about it, she explained that it was the pie you made in the years that a pecan crop was poor; in other words, a pecan pie without the pecans. You line the crust with a layer of tart jelly before adding the filling, and the tart flavor is a nice complement to the sweet. I was never able to discover the provenance of the name.

1	unbaked piecrust
1/3	cup salted butter
3	large eggs
1	cup cane syrup or dark corn syrup
2/3	cup granulated sugar
1/4	cup crab apple or red currant jelly, or any tart jelly

Preheat your oven to 350°F.

In a small saucepan, melt the butter. In a medium bowl, whisk the eggs until they are light in color. Add the syrup, the sugar, and the butter, and whisk the ingredients until they are well combined.

Line the piecrust with the jelly, then pour the filling into the piecrust.

Place the pie in the oven, and bake it until the filling is set in the middle, about 35 minutes.

Pecan Pie

This is a Southern specialty. If you are lucky enough to find the Texas native pecans, use those. The nut meats are small, but sweet and extremely flavorful. Black walnut pie and hickory nut pie are interesting variations, made by simply substituting black walnuts or hickory nuts for the pecans.

1	unbaked piecrust
1/3	cup salted butter
3	large eggs
1	cup cane syrup or dark corn syrup
2/3	cup granulated sugar
1	cup pecan halves or pieces

Preheat your oven to 350°F.

In a small saucepan, melt the butter. In a medium bowl, whisk the eggs until they are light. Add the syrup, the sugar, and the butter, and whisk the ingredients until they are well combined. Stir in the pecans, then pour the filling into the piecrust.

Place the pie in the oven, and bake it until the filling is set in the middle, about 35 minutes.

Butternut Maple Pie

This is the Northern cousin to pecan pie. Butternuts grow wild in New England and other parts of the Eastern United States; as they are increasingly difficult to find, Persian walnuts, which are related, can be used instead to make a maple walnut pie.

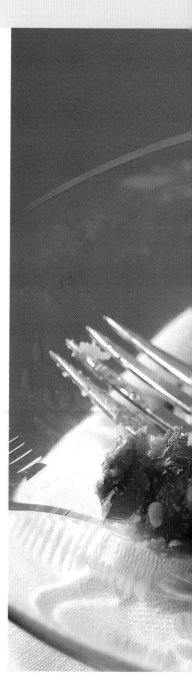

1	unbaked piecrust
1	cup butternuts or walnuts
1½	cups pure maple syrup
2	tablespoons salted butter
3	large eggs
¼	cup packed light brown sugar

Preheat your oven to 350°F.

Break the nuts into pieces.

Pour the syrup into at least a 3-quart saucepan and bring it to a boil over medium heat. Let it boil down until you have 1 cup, about 8 minutes, stirring it down as needed. Keep a teaspoon of the butter handy. If the syrup looks about to boil over, toss in the piece of butter. Remove the syrup from the heat and allow it to cool.

In a small saucepan, melt the butter. In a medium bowl, whisk the eggs until they are light in color. Add the syrup, the sugar, and the butter, and whisk the ingredients until they are combined. Stir in the nuts, then pour the filling into the piecrust.

Place the pie in the oven, and bake it until the filling is set in the middle, about 35 minutes.

Osgood Pie

One theory holds that the original name of this was O-so-good pie. You will also find it called Allgood pie. Unlike with other transparent pies, the eggs are separated, with the whites whipped and folded in at the end.

1	unbaked piecrust
½	cup pecans or walnuts
2	large eggs, separated
½	cup granulated sugar
4	tablespoons salted butter
½	teaspoon ground cinnamon
½	teaspoon ground nutmeg
1	tablespoon white vinegar
½	cup raisins

Preheat your oven to 350°F.

Break or chop the nuts into pieces.

Separate the eggs, placing the yolks in a small bowl, and the whites in a large bowl.

In a medium bowl, cream the sugar and butter. Beat in the egg yolks. Add the spices and the vinegar, then stir in the raisins and the nuts.

Whisk the egg whites until they are stiff, then fold them into the raisin mixture. Pour the filling into the piecrust.

Place the pie in the oven, and bake it until the filling is set in the middle, and golden brown on the top, about 30 minutes.

Boiled Cider Pie

The **Yankee Cook Book** *says boiled cider pie is as traditional as New England boiled dinner. Although no longer widely available, boiled cider is still made by a few producers, and this recipe includes instructions for making your own.*

1 unbaked piecrust
6 cups unpasteurized apple cider, or 1½ cups prepared boiled cider, such as Wood's Cider Mill
3 large eggs
1 cup whole milk
½ cup maple syrup or granulated sugar
¼ cup unbleached all-purpose flour

Preheat your oven to 350°F.

Pour the cider into a large kettle. (To be able to properly gauge what 1½ cups will look like in the pot, pour in that much uncooked cider first, then add the remainder.) Bring it to a boil over high heat. Reduce the heat to low and simmer, uncovered, for 4 hours, or until the mixture is reduced to 1½ cups.

In a large bowl, whisk the eggs until they are light in color. Add the cider, the milk, the syrup or sugar, and the flour, and stir the ingredients until they are well combined. Pour the filling into the piecrust.

Place the pie in the oven, and bake it until the filling is set in the middle, about 45 minutes.

Vinegar Pie

This pie was made at the end of winter, when the larder was nearly empty. It has a surprisingly fruity taste.

1   unbaked piecrust
2   large eggs
1   cup granulated sugar
¾   cup water
3   tablespoons white vinegar
2   tablespoons unbleached all-purpose flour

Preheat your oven to 350°F.

In a medium bowl, whisk the eggs until they are light in color. Add the sugar, the water, the vinegar, and the flour, and stir the ingredients until they are well combined. Pour the filling into the piecrust.

Place the pie in the oven and bake it until the filling is set in the middle, about 35 minutes.

Chess Pie

A very old man told me that these "newfangled" lemon chess pies were not the chess pies he grew up eating. This is the one I made for him, and it met with his approval.

1   unbaked piecrust
½   cup salted butter
3   large eggs
1   cup granulated sugar
2   tablespoons yellow cornmeal

Preheat your oven to 350°F.

In a small saucepan, melt the butter. In a medium bowl, whisk the eggs until they are light in color. Add the sugar, the butter, and the cornmeal, and stir the ingredients until they are just combined. Pour the filling into the piecrust.

Place the pie in the oven, and bake it until the filling is set in the middle, about 35 minutes.

Lemon Chess Pie

Here is the "newfangled" version of chess pie, although this recipe dates to before 1900.

- 1 unbaked piecrust
- 1 medium lemon, or ¼ cup lemon juice
- ½ cup salted butter
- 3 large eggs
- 1 cup granulated sugar
- 2 tablespoons yellow cornmeal

Preheat your oven to 350°F.

Juice the lemon, measuring out ¼ cup.

In a small saucepan, melt the butter. In a medium bowl, whisk the eggs until they are light in color. Add the sugar, the butter, the cornmeal, and the lemon juice, and stir the ingredients until they are just combined.

Pour the filling into the piecrust.

Place the pie in the oven, and bake it until the filling is set in the middle, about 35 minutes.

Buttermilk Pie

Buttermilk was the liquid left in the churn after butter was made. Because milk had to sit for the cream to rise, natural fermentation began, which was what gave buttermilk its characteristic tangy flavor. (Modern buttermilk is cultured, much like yogurt.)

1	unbaked piecrust
½	cup salted butter
3	large eggs
1	cup granulated sugar
¼	cup unbleached all-purpose flour
1	cup buttermilk
⅛	teaspoon ground nutmeg

Preheat your oven to 350°F.

In a small saucepan, melt the butter. In a medium bowl, whisk the eggs until they are light in color. Add the sugar, the butter, and the flour, and whisk the ingredients until they are well combined. Fold in the buttermilk and nutmeg. Pour the filling into the piecrust.

Place the pie in the oven, and bake it until the filling is set in the middle, about 30 minutes.

Tears on Your Pillow Pie

This simple recipe is from the Amish, and it makes a very thin pie. The origin of its name seems to be a mystery, but one theory is that it was made to console someone who had been disappointed by a sweetheart.

1	unbaked piecrust
⅓	cup salted butter
2	large eggs
1½	cups packed light brown sugar
¼	cup whole milk
¼	cup heavy cream
1	tablespoon unbleached all-purpose flour

Preheat your oven to 350°F.

In a small saucepan, melt the butter. In a medium bowl, whisk the eggs until they are light in color. Add the brown sugar, the butter, the milk, the cream, and the flour, and whisk the ingredients until they are well combined. Pour the filling into the piecrust.

Place the pie in the oven, and bake it until the filling is set in the middle, about 35 minutes.

Transparent Pie, *Kentucky Style*

Don't confuse this with the modern-day pie called Kentucky or Derby pie, which contains chocolate chips. This old recipe comes from eastern Kentucky.

1	unbaked piecrust
2	large eggs
1½	cups granulated sugar
½	cup salted butter
2	tablespoons unbleached all-purpose flour
1	cup heavy cream
1	teaspoon vanilla extract

Preheat your oven to 350°F.

In a medium bowl, whisk the eggs until they are light in color.

In a medium bowl, cream the sugar and the butter. Beat in the eggs, then the flour. Stir in the cream and the vanilla. Pour the filling into the piecrust.

Place the pie in the oven, and bake it until the filling is set in the middle, about 45 minutes.

Jefferson Davis Pie

Culinary historians believe that a Missouri slave named Mary Ann invented this pie during the Civil War, when she worked as a cook for a Confederate merchant. It varies from other transparent pies by the addition of a meringue topping.

1 partially baked piecrust (see page 18)
6 large dates
½ cup pecans
4 large eggs
2 cups packed light brown sugar
½ cup salted butter
2 tablespoons unbleached all-purpose flour
1 teaspoon ground cinnamon
1 teaspoon ground nutmeg
½ teaspoon ground allspice
1 cup heavy cream
½ cup raisins
⅛ teaspoon salt
6 tablespoons granulated sugar

Preheat your oven to 350°F.

Chop the dates and measure out ½ cup. Break the pecans into pieces.

Separate the eggs, placing the yolks in a small bowl, and the whites in a large bowl. Lightly whisk the egg yolks.

In a medium bowl, cream the brown sugar and the butter. Beat in the egg yolks. Add the flour and the spices. Stir in the cream, the dates, the raisins, and the nuts. Pour the filling into the piecrust.

Place the pie in the oven, with a rimmed baking sheet under it in case it bubbles over, and bake it until the filling is set in the middle, about 45 minutes. While the pie is cooling, make the meringue.

Using a clean whisk, whisk the egg whites with the salt until the mixture is stiff. Gradually beat in the granulated sugar until the mixture is glossy and the sugar is dissolved. To determine if the sugar is dissolved, rub a bit of the meringue between your fingers. If it feels gritty, beat it for a minute longer, then test it again.

Spread the meringue evenly over the pie filling, and seal it to the crust. Place the pie in the oven, and bake it for 20 minutes, or until the meringue is delicately browned.

Stack Pie

Stack pie dates back to colonial days. When people went visiting, they brought food, and needed something that traveled well. Space was also at a premium, so stacking pies and holding them together with icing was the answer. Three to five pies, or sometimes even six, were baked with a shallow filling and stacked, with a thin layer of icing spread between them. You will want to serve very *thin slices of this.*

4	unbaked piecrusts
5	large eggs
1½	cups plus 3 tablespoons salted butter, divided
3	cups granulated sugar
1½	teaspoons vanilla extract, divided
2	cups plus 2 tablespoons heavy cream, divided
2	cups packed light brown sugar
⅛	teaspoon salt

Trim the piecrusts so that the rims of your pie plates are exposed.

Preheat your oven to 350°F.

In a small saucepan, melt 1½ cups of the butter.

Whisk the eggs until they are light. Add the granulated sugar, the melted butter, and ½ teaspoon of the vanilla, and whisk until well combined. Fold in 1 cup of the cream. Pour 1½ cups of the filling into each piecrust.

Place the pies in the oven, two or four, as room allows, and bake them until the filling is set in the middle, about 35 minutes. Allow the pies to cool in the pie plates. While the pies are cooling, make the icing.

In a large saucepan, combine 1 cup of the cream, the brown sugar, and the salt. Stir until the sugar is dissolved. Over medium-high heat, bring

the mixture to a soft boil. Cook it for 5 minutes, without stirring, until the mixture thickens a bit, or reaches 238°F on a candy thermometer. Remove the saucepan from the heat, stir in the remaining 3 tablespoons of butter, and let the mixture cool for 15 minutes. Stir in the remaining teaspoon of vanilla.

Beat the icing until it is thick and creamy. If the icing seems too firm to spread, beat in additional cream, 1 tablespoon at a time.

Run a long, thin spatula around and under one of the pies to slip it out of its pan. Place it on a cake dish or large plate, and spread the top lightly with about ½ cup of the icing.

Stack the second pie on top of the first, and spread the top with about ½ cup of the icing. Repeat with the third pie. Stack the fourth pie on top. Frost it with the remaining icing.

Cake pies are a Pennsylvania Dutch specialty. They were really just variations on transparent pie, but the finished product is so different that I thought they warranted their own section. In traditional Pennsylvania Dutch baking, molasses and lard were often used in place of sugar and butter.

CHAPTER THREE

Cake Pies

Shoofly Pie

This pie is probably the one most identified with Pennsylvania Dutch pastry making. There are two variations, dry-bottom and wet-bottom. Dry bottom shoofly has a cakelike texture under the crumb topping, whereas wet bottom produces a more custardlike result. Many modern recipes include eggs, but eggs were expensive in the 19th century, chickens didn't lay in the winter, and a pie without eggs had a longer shelf life. So these two recipes don't include them.

Dry-Bottom

1	unbaked piecrust
1½	cups unbleached all-purpose flour
½	cup packed light brown sugar
½	cup lard or solid vegetable shortening
½	cup unsulfured molasses (not blackstrap)
½	cup boiling water
1	teaspoon baking soda

Preheat your oven to 350°F.

In a medium bowl, combine the flour and sugar with a fork. With a pastry blender or two knives, very lightly and quickly cut the lard into the flour mixture to form crumbs about the size of peas.

Pour the molasses into a separate medium bowl. In a 2-cup glass measure, dissolve the baking soda in the boiling water, then immediately pour it into the molasses. Stir the molasses mixture until it is smooth.

Stir the crumb mixture into the molasses mixture, then pour the filling into the piecrust.

Place the pie in the oven, and bake it until the filling is set in the middle, about 40 minutes.

OPPOSITE: **Dry-Bottom Shoofly Pie**

Wet-Bottom

1	unbaked piecrust
1	cup unbleached all-purpose flour
½	cup packed light brown sugar
¼	cup lard or solid vegetable shortening
1	cup unsulfured molasses (not blackstrap)
¾	cup boiling water
½	teaspoon baking soda

Preheat your oven to 350°F.

In a medium bowl, combine the flour and sugar with a fork. With a pastry blender or two knives, very lightly and quickly cut the lard into the flour mixture to form crumbs about the size of peas.

Pour the molasses into a separate medium bowl. In a 2-cup glass measure, dissolve the baking soda in the boiling water, then immediately pour it

into the molasses. Stir the molasses mixture until it is smooth.

ABOVE: **Wet-Bottom Shoofly Pie**

Pour the molasses mixture into the piecrust, then sprinkle the crumb mixture evenly over the top.

Place the pie in the oven, and bake it until the filling is set in the middle, about 40 minutes.

Quakertown Pie

This very moist pie is similar to wet-bottom shoofly pie.

  1   unbaked piecrust
  1   large egg
  ½   cup unsulfured molasses (not blackstrap)
  1   cup plus 2 tablespoons unbleached all-purpose flour, divided
1½   cups water
1¼   teaspoons vanilla extract
  ⅓   cup packed light brown sugar
  ½   teaspoon baking soda
  ⅛   teaspoon ground cinnamon
  ¼   cup lard

Preheat your oven to 350°F.

In a small bowl, whisk the egg until it is light in color.

In a medium saucepan, combine the molasses with the egg and 2 tablespoons of the flour. Slowly stir in the water. Bring the mixture to a boil over medium heat, stirring it constantly, then, still stirring, let it boil for 1 minute. Remove the saucepan from the heat, and stir in the vanilla. Allow the molasses mixture to cool to room temperature.

While the molasses mixture is cooling, in a medium bowl, combine the remaining cup of flour, the brown sugar, the baking soda, and the cinnamon. With a pastry cutter or two knives, very lightly and quickly cut the lard into the flour mixture to form crumbs about the size of peas.

Pour the molasses mixture into the piecrust, then sprinkle the crumbs evenly over the filling.

Place the pie in the oven, and bake it until the filling is set in the middle, about 40 minutes.

Crumb Pie

This recipe, and the one for gravel pie, makes use of the crumbs left over from cookies or cakes. These were recipes for a thrifty and provident housewife, one who made sure that nothing in her kitchen went to waste.

1	unbaked piecrust
½	cup raisins
3	large eggs
1	cup unsulfured molasses (not blackstrap)
½	cup hot water (120°F)
1	cup fine cookie or cake crumbs
⅓	cup unbleached all-purpose flour
1	teaspoon ground cinnamon
¼	teaspoon ground nutmeg
⅛	teaspoon ground ginger
⅓	cup lard

Preheat your oven to 350°F.

Sprinkle the bottom of the piecrust with the raisins.

In a small bowl, whisk the eggs until they are light in color.

In a medium saucepan, combine the molasses with the hot water and the eggs. Cook the mixture over low heat, stirring it constantly, until it is smooth and thick, about 5 minutes. Remove the saucepan from the heat, and allow the molasses mixture to cool to room temperature.

While the molasses mixture is cooling, combine, in a medium bowl, the cookie crumbs, the flour, and the spices. With a pastry blender or two knives, very lightly and quickly cut the lard into the crumb mixture to form crumbs about the size of peas.

Pour the molasses mixture over the raisins, then sprinkle the crumbs evenly over the filling.

Place the pie in the oven, and bake it until the filling is set in the middle, about 40 minutes.

Gravel Pie

Gravel pie uses the same ingredients as crumb pie, but the method of preparation is different, with the crumbs and spices layered over the cooked filling.

1	unbaked piecrust
½	cup raisins
3	large eggs
1	cup unsulfured molasses (not blackstrap)
½	cup hot water (120°F)
⅓	cup unbleached all-purpose flour
⅓	cup lard
1	cup fine cookie or cake crumbs
1	teaspoon ground cinnamon
¼	teaspoon ground nutmeg
⅛	teaspoon ground ginger

Preheat your oven to 350°F.

Sprinkle the bottom of the piecrust with the raisins.

In a small bowl, whisk the eggs until they are light in color.

In a medium saucepan, combine the molasses with the hot water and the eggs. Cook the mixture over low heat, stirring it constantly, until it is smooth and thick, about 5 minutes. Remove the saucepan from the heat, and allow the molasses mixture to cool to room temperature.

While the molasses mixture is cooling, place the flour in a medium bowl. With a pastry blender or two knives, very lightly and quickly cut the lard into the flour to form crumbs about the size of peas.

Pour the molasses mixture over the raisins.

Set aside ¼ cup of the cookie crumbs. Sprinkle the remaining crumbs over the filling, then the flour mixture, then the spices. Sprinkle the ¼ cup of reserved crumbs over the top.

Place the pie in the oven, and bake it until the filling is set in the middle, about 40 minutes.

Amish Vanilla Pie

This wet-bottom crumb pie is flavored with vanilla instead of spices.

1	unbaked piecrust
1	large egg
¾	cup unsulfured molasses (not blackstrap)
1	cup plus 1 tablespoon unbleached all-purpose flour, divided
1	cup water
1½	teaspoons vanilla extract
½	cup packed light brown sugar
½	teaspoon cream of tartar
½	teaspoon baking soda
⅛	teaspoon salt
¼	cup lard

Preheat your oven to 350°F.

In a small bowl, whisk the egg until it is light in color.

In a medium saucepan, combine the molasses with the egg and 1 table-spoon of the flour. Slowly stir in the water. Bring the mixture to a boil over medium heat, stirring it constantly, then, still stirring, let it boil for 1 minute. Remove the saucepan from the heat, and stir in the vanilla. Allow the molasses mixture to cool to room temperature.

While the molasses mixture is cooling, in a medium bowl, combine the remaining cup of flour, the brown sugar, the cream of tartar, the baking soda, and the salt. With a pastry cutter or two knives, very lightly and quickly cut the lard into the flour mixture to form crumbs about the size of peas.

Pour the molasses mixture into the piecrust, then sprinkle the crumbs evenly over the filling.

Place the pie in the oven, and bake it until the filling is set in the middle, about 40 minutes.

Funny Cake

There are no crumbs in this pie, but it has a moist, chocolate bottom layer. The "funny" bit refers to the way the chocolate layer is on top when the pie goes into the oven, but on the bottom when it comes out.

1	unbaked piecrust
1	large egg
1	cup unsulfured molasses (not blackstrap)
¼	cup lard
½	cup whole milk
1	cup unbleached all-purpose flour
1	teaspoon baking powder
½	teaspoon plus ¼ teaspoon vanilla extract, divided
½	cup granulated sugar
¼	cup unsweetened cocoa powder
¼	cup plus 2 tablespoons water

Preheat your oven to 350°F.

In a small bowl, lightly whisk the egg.

In a large bowl, cream the molasses with the lard. Stir in the egg, then the milk. Add the flour and the baking powder, and beat the batter until it is smooth. Stir in ½ teaspoon of the vanilla, then pour the filling into the piecrust.

In a medium bowl, mix together the sugar and the cocoa powder. Stir in the water and the remaining ¼ teaspoon of vanilla. Pour the cocoa mixture carefully over the top of the batter.

Place the pie in the oven, and bake it until a toothpick inserted in the center of the top layer comes out clean, about 40 minutes.

Montgomery Pie

This pie originated in Montgomery County, Pennsylvania. It has the same sort of structure as Funny Cake, but the top (then bottom) layer is a lemony molasses. It dates from a time when lemons were expensive and considered a rare treat.

1	unbaked piecrust
1	medium lemon
2	large eggs
¾	cup unsulfured molasses (not blackstrap)
¾	cup hot water (120°F)
1¼	cups unbleached all-purpose flour
½	teaspoon baking soda
½	teaspoon salt
¼	cup lard
⅔	cup granulated sugar
½	cup sour milk or buttermilk

Preheat your oven to 350°F.

Zest and juice the lemon. Measure out 1 tablespoon of the zest and 3 tablespoons of the juice.

In a small bowl, lightly whisk one of the eggs.

In a medium bowl, combine the molasses, the hot water, the beaten egg, and the lemon juice and rind. Mix them well.

In another medium bowl, combine the flour with the baking soda and the salt.

In the same small bowl lightly whisk the remaining egg. In a large bowl, cream the lard with the sugar, then mix in the egg well.

Add the flour mixture, alternating with the milk, to the sugar mixture.

Pour the filling into the pie shell, then cover it evenly with the molasses mixture.

Place the pie in the oven, and bake it until a toothpick inserted in the center of the top layer comes out clean, about 45 minutes.

CHAPTER FOUR

Custard Pies

Custard pie made its first appearance in American cookbooks nearly 200 years ago. Milk, sugar, and eggs were the usual basis for a custard, and the recipes in this chapter, with one notable exception, make use of them.

Custard Pie

Made with ingredients almost everyone would have had on hand, this custard pie is an old-fashioned exercise in thrift.

- 1 partially baked piecrust (see page 18)
- 3 large eggs
- 2 cups whole milk
- ½ cup granulated sugar
- 1 teaspoon vanilla extract
- ¼ teaspoon salt
- ¼ teaspoon ground nutmeg

Preheat your oven to 350°F.

In a medium bowl whisk the eggs until they are light in color. Add the milk, the sugar, the vanilla, and the salt, and whisk the ingredients until they are well combined. Pour the filling into the piecrust, and sprinkle the top with the nutmeg.

Place the pie in the oven, and bake it until the filling is set in the middle, about 30 minutes.

Bob Andy Pie

This pie has its roots in the Amish communities of the Midwest. The common story behind the name: an Amish farmer after tasting this pie said it was "as good as Bob and Andy," his two prize plow horses. As the custard bakes, some of the cinnamon sinks to the bottom, giving this pie a layered look when sliced.

1	unbaked piecrust
3	large eggs
2	cups whole milk
1	cup granulated sugar
2	tablespoons unbleached all-purpose flour
2	teaspoons ground cinnamon
½	teaspoon salt

Preheat your oven to 350°F.

In a medium bowl, whisk the eggs until they are light in color. Whisk in the milk.

In a small bowl, combine the sugar, the flour, the cinnamon, and the salt, then whisk the ingredients into the egg mixture. Pour the filling into the piecrust.

Place the pie in the oven, and bake it until the filling is set in the middle, about 40 minutes.

Sugar Cream Pie

A sort-of custard pie, but without the eggs. It's also known as Hoosier pie, Indiana cream pie, and finger pie, the last because, traditionally, you mixed the ingredients directly in the crust with your finger. Although this pie is associated with the Amish, it actually predates their arrival and may have originated with Quaker settlers who came to Indiana from North Carolina in the early nineteenth century. It was adopted as the official state pie of Indiana in 2009.

1	unbaked piecrust
1	cup granulated sugar
2	tablespoons unbleached all-purpose flour
⅛	teaspoon salt
1	cup heavy cream
¾	cup whole milk
⅛	teaspoon ground nutmeg

Preheat your oven to 350°F.

To make this in the traditional way, mix the sugar, the flour, and the salt directly in the piecrust, using your finger. Pour the cream and the milk over the sugar mixture. Again, with your finger, gently stir the ingredients until they are combined, taking care not to break the crust. Sprinkle the nutmeg over the top.

Or, if you don't want "a finger in every pie," in a medium bowl, combine the sugar, the flour, and the salt, then sprinkle it evenly over the bottom of the piecrust. Combine the cream and the milk, and pour them over the sugar mixture. Stir the ingredients with a wooden spoon, gently, so as not to break the crust, then sprinkle the nutmeg over the top.

Place the pie in the oven, and bake it until the filling is almost set in the middle, about 50 minutes. You must let this pie cool completely before cutting it, or the filling will run.

Union Pie

This custard pie comes from Pennsylvania Dutch country. Like many of the desserts from that region, it is flavored with molasses.

1	unbaked piecrust
2	large eggs
½	cup granulated sugar
½	cup whole milk
½	cup unsulfured molasses (not blackstrap)
½	cup buttermilk
¼	teaspoon baking soda
1	tablespoon unbleached all-purpose flour
½	teaspoon vanilla extract
⅛	teaspoon salt

Preheat your oven to 350°F.

In a large bowl, whisk the eggs until they are light in color. Add the remaining ingredients and mix them well, then pour the filling into the piecrust.

Place the pie in the oven, and bake it until the filling is set in the middle, about 30 minutes.

Marlborough Pie

This apple custard is one of the oldest American pies. It was a popular dish served during the holidays in 18th- and 19th-century New England.

1   unbaked piecrust
1   large apple
1   medium lemon, or 3 tablespoons lemon juice
3   large eggs
⅓   cup granulated sugar
⅔   cup whole milk

Preheat your oven to 350°F.

Core and pare the apple, then grate it. Juice the lemon, straining out the seeds and pulp.

In a small bowl, whisk the eggs until they are light in color. In a large bowl, combine the apple with the sugar, the milk, and the lemon juice. Stir in the eggs, then pour the filling into the piecrust.

Place the pie in the oven, and bake it until the filling is set in the middle, about 25 minutes.

Squash Pie

Squash is one of the Three Sisters, with maize and beans, of Native American agriculture, and was one of the first foods introduced by Native Americans to the European settlers. Pumpkin has become the most popular of the squashes used for pie, but, in Colonial America, any of the winter squashes would have been used. Hubbard, butternut, and acorn all produce a fantastic pie.

1	unbaked piecrust
1	(2½- to 3-pound) winter squash, or 1 (15-ounce) can squash puree
2	large eggs
¾	cup granulated sugar
½	teaspoon salt
1	teaspoon ground cinnamon
½	teaspoon ground ginger
¼	teaspoon ground nutmeg
¼	teaspoon ground allspice
¾	cup whole milk
¾	cup heavy cream

If you're using canned squash, skip to the next paragraph. Otherwise, split the squash in half with a heavy knife or a cleaver. Clean out the seeds and stringy pulp. Place the squash pieces, cut side down, in a steaming basket over simmering water. Cover the pot and steam the squash for 1 hour, or until it is very soft. Scrape the flesh free from the rind, and mash it until it is very smooth. Place the mashed squash in a colander for 30 minutes to 1 hour, until it is well drained, then measure out 2 cups.

Preheat your oven to 350°F.

In a medium bowl, whisk the eggs until they are light in color. Add the squash, the sugar, and the salt, and whisk the ingredients until they are well combined. Stir in the spices. Fold in the milk and the cream. Pour the filling into the piecrust.

Place the pie in the oven, and bake it until the filling is set in the middle, about 45 minutes.

If you have too much filling for the piecrust, pour the remainder into a custard dish and bake it while the pie is baking.

Pumpkin Pie

This recipe produces a strongly spiced pumpkin pie. For a milder version, just cut the quantities of spices in half.

- 1 unbaked piecrust
- 1 (2½- to 3-pound) pie pumpkin, or 1 (15-ounce) can pure pumpkin puree
- 2 large eggs
- ¾ cup granulated sugar
- ½ teaspoon salt
- 2 teaspoons ground cinnamon
- 1 teaspoon ground ginger
- 1 teaspoon ground nutmeg
- ½ teaspoon ground allspice
- ½ teaspoon ground mace
- ¼ teaspoon ground cloves
- ¾ cup whole milk
- ¾ cup heavy cream

If you're using canned pumpkin, skip to the next paragraph. Otherwise, split the pumpkin in half with a heavy knife or a cleaver. Cut out the stem and clean out the stringy pulp. Place the pumpkin pieces, cut side down, in a steaming basket over simmering water. Cover the pot and steam the pumpkin for 1 hour, or until it is very soft. Scrape the flesh free from the rind, and mash it until it is very smooth. Place the mashed pumpkin in a colander for 30 minutes to 1 hour, until it is well drained, then measure out 2 cups.

Preheat your oven to 350°F.

In a medium bowl, whisk the eggs until they are light in color. Add the pumpkin, the sugar, and the salt, and whisk the ingredients until they are well combined. Stir in the spices. Fold in the milk and the cream.

Pour the filling into the piecrust.

Place the pie in the oven, and bake it until the filling is set in the middle, about 45 minutes.

Sweet Potato Pie

While northerners were making squash pies in colonial times, southerners were making sweet potato pies. (Sweet potatoes grow well in humid southern climates and winter squashes do not.) Like winter squash, sweet potatoes were introduced to European settlers by the Native Americans.

1	unbaked piecrust
1½	pounds sweet potatoes (about 4 large), or 1 (15-ounce) can sweet potato puree
2	large eggs
¾	cup granulated sugar
½	teaspoon salt
½	teaspoon ground nutmeg
¾	cup whole milk
¾	cup heavy cream

If you're using canned sweet potato puree, skip to the next paragraph. Peel the sweet potatoes deeply, removing both the skin and the fibrous layer beneath it. Cut the potatoes into 1-inch chunks, then place them in a stockpot and cover them with cold water. Bring the water to a boil, and cook, uncovered, for 20 minutes, or until the potatoes are very tender. Drain them well, then mash them until they are smooth. Measure out 2 cups.

Preheat your oven to 350°F.

In a medium bowl, whisk the eggs until they are light in color. Add the sweet potato, the sugar, and the salt, and whisk the ingredients until they are well combined. Stir in the nutmeg. Fold in the milk and the cream. Pour the filling into the piecrust.

Place the pie in the oven, and bake it until the filling is set in the middle, about 45 minutes.

CHAPTER FIVE

Cream Pies

Nowadays, we think of cream pie as having a pudding-like filling (thickened with egg yolks) and a whipped cream topping. In the old days, a cream pie had a meringue topping. That was because, in early kitchens, making a meringue of the egg whites ensured that nothing went to waste. However, any of the pies in this section, with the exception of the lemon, can be prepared without the meringue. (The lemon filling, without the protection of a meringue, will form a gummy layer as it oxidizes.) Cream pies (with meringue topping) date to at least the 18th century in America.

If you can, try to make your pie on a dry day, as humidity can cause the meringue to weep. If you can't, the pie will still be delicious.

Cream Pie

This was the most basic of the cream pies, but one you rarely find anymore.

1 prebaked piecrust (see page 18)
3 large eggs
¾ cup plus 6 tablespoons granulated sugar, divided
½ cup unbleached all-purpose flour
¼ teaspoon plus ⅛ teaspoon salt, divided
2½ cups whole milk
1 tablespoon salted butter
1 teaspoon vanilla extract

MAKING CREAM PIE FILLING

TOP LEFT: **chocolate custard cooked to proper consistency**

TOP RIGHT: **tempering the egg yolks**

BOTTOM: **pouring cooked chocolate custard into prebaked pie shell**

Separate the eggs, placing the yolks in a 2-cup glass measure, and the whites in a large mixing bowl.

In a large saucepan, combine ¾ cup of the sugar, the flour, and ¼ teaspoon of the salt.

In a separate pan, scald the milk, and then pour it over the dry ingredients, stirring them constantly until everything is well mixed. Place the large saucepan over medium heat, and cook the milk mixture, stirring it constantly, until it is smooth and thick, about 2 minutes. Remove it from the heat.

Whisk the egg yolks well, then stir about ½ cup of the hot milk mixture into them. Stir the yolk mixture back into the saucepan. Return the saucepan to medium heat and, stirring the filling constantly, bring it to a boil, then cook it for 1 minute.

To avoid a runny filling, this additional minute of cooking is important. If it's not done, amylase, an enzyme in the egg yolk, will react with the starch in the flour and thin out the filling.

Remove the filling from the heat, and stir in the butter and the vanilla.

Pour the warm filling into the piecrust, and allow it to cool while you make your meringue.

Preheat your oven to 350°F.

Using a clean whisk, whisk the egg whites with the remaining ⅛ teaspoon of salt until the mixture is stiff. Gradually beat in the remaining 6 tablespoons of sugar until the mixture is glossy, and the sugar is dissolved. To determine whether the sugar is dissolved, rub a bit of the meringue between your fingers. If it feels gritty, beat it for a minute longer, then test it again.

Spread the meringue evenly over the pie filling, and seal it to the crust.

Place the pie in the oven, and bake it for 20 minutes, or until the meringue is delicately browned.

MAKING MERINGUE

ABOVE LEFT: **properly whipped meringue**

ABOVE RIGHT: **placing meringue on filling**

OPPOSITE PAGE
TOP LEFT: **spreading meringue**

TOP RIGHT: **sealing meringue to edges**

BOTTOM: **finished meringue**

Butterscotch Cream Pie

Butterscotch was developed as a candy in the early 1800s in England. The flavor combination of brown sugar and butter was so popular that it soon made its way into other dishes.

1	prebaked piecrust (see page 18)
3	large eggs
¾	cup packed light brown sugar
½	cup unbleached all-purpose flour
¼	teaspoon plus ⅛ teaspoon salt, divided
2½	cups whole milk
4	tablespoons salted butter
1	teaspoon vanilla extract
6	tablespoons granulated sugar

Separate the eggs, placing the yolks in a 2-cup glass measure, and the whites in a large mixing bowl.

In a large saucepan, combine the brown sugar, the flour, and ¼ teaspoon of the salt.

In a separate pan, scald the milk, and then pour it over the dry ingredients, stirring them constantly until everything is well mixed. Place the large saucepan over medium heat, and cook the milk mixture, stirring it constantly, until it is smooth and thick, about 2 minutes. Remove it from the heat.

Whisk the egg yolks well, then stir about ½ cup of the hot milk mixture into them. Stir the yolk mixture back into the saucepan. Return the saucepan to medium heat and, stirring the filling constantly, bring it to a boil, then cook it for 1 minute.

To avoid a runny filling, this additional minute of cooking is important. If it's not done, amylase, an enzyme in the egg yolk, will react with the starch in the flour and thin out the filling.

Remove the filling from the heat, and stir in the butter and the vanilla.

Pour the warm filling into the piecrust, and allow it to cool while you make your meringue.

Preheat your oven to 350°F.

Using a clean whisk, whisk the egg whites with the remaining ⅛ teaspoon of salt until the mixture is stiff. Gradually beat in the granulated sugar until the mixture is glossy, and the sugar is dissolved. To determine whether the sugar is dissolved, rub a bit of the meringue between your fingers. If it feels gritty, beat it for a minute longer, then test it again.

Spread the meringue evenly over the pie filling, and seal it to the crust. Place the pie in the oven, and bake it for 20 minutes, or until the meringue is delicately browned.

Chocolate Cream Pie

In colonial America, cocoa was used in both beverages and puddings, as single-crust pies were then known. A British report dating from 1682 detailed cocoa exports from Jamaica to Boston.

1	prebaked piecrust (see page 18)
3	large eggs
¾	cup plus 6 tablespoons granulated sugar, divided
⅓	cup unbleached all-purpose flour
¼	cup unsweetened cocoa powder
¼	teaspoon plus ⅛ teaspoon salt, divided
2½	cups whole milk
1	tablespoon salted butter
1	teaspoon vanilla extract

Separate the eggs, placing the yolks in a 2-cup glass measure, and the whites in a large mixing bowl.

In a large saucepan, combine ¾ cup of the sugar, the flour, the cocoa, and ¼ teaspoon of the salt.

In a separate pan, scald the milk, and then pour it over the dry ingredients, stirring them constantly until everything is well mixed. Place the large saucepan over medium heat, and cook the milk mixture, stirring it constantly, until it is smooth and thick, about 2 minutes. Remove it from the heat.

Whisk the egg yolks well, then stir about ½ cup of the hot milk mixture into them. Stir the yolk mixture back into the saucepan. Return the saucepan to medium heat and, stirring the filling constantly, bring it to a boil, then cook it for 1 minute.

To avoid a runny filling, this additional minute of cooking is important. If it's not done, amylase, an enzyme in the egg yolk, will react with the starch in the flour and thin out the filling.

Remove the filling from the heat, and stir in the butter and the vanilla.

Pour the warm filling into the piecrust, and allow it to cool while you make your meringue.

Preheat your oven to 350°F.

Using a clean whisk, whisk the egg whites with the remaining ⅛ teaspoon of salt until the mixture is stiff. Gradually beat in the remaining 6 tablespoons of sugar until the mixture is glossy, and the sugar is dissolved. To determine whether the sugar is dissolved, rub a bit of the meringue between your fingers. If it feels gritty, beat it for a minute longer, then test it again.

Spread the meringue evenly over the pie filling, and seal it to the crust. Place the pie in the oven, and bake it for 20 minutes, or until the meringue is delicately browned.

Coconut Cream Pie

In 1895, Franklin Baker, a Philadelphia flour miller, received a cargo of coconuts from Cuba in payment for a consignment of flour. When he was unable to sell them, he set up a factory for shredding and drying the coconut meat. Soon, coconut desserts were all the rage. You'll find coconut spelled "cocoanut" in old recipe books.

1	prebaked piecrust (see page 18)
3	large eggs
¾	cup plus 6 tablespoons granulated sugar, divided
½	cup unbleached all-purpose flour
¼	teaspoon plus ⅛ teaspoon salt, divided
2½	cups whole milk
1	tablespoon salted butter
1	teaspoon vanilla extract
½	cup plus ¼ cup unsweetened shredded coconut, divided

Separate the eggs, placing the yolks in a 2-cup glass measure, and the whites in a large mixing bowl.

In a large saucepan, combine ¾ cup of the sugar, the flour, and ¼ teaspoon of the salt.

In a separate pan, scald the milk, and then pour it over the dry ingredients, stirring them constantly until everything is well mixed. Place the large saucepan over medium heat, and cook the milk mixture, stirring it constantly, until it is smooth and thick, about 2 minutes. Remove it from the heat.

Whisk the egg yolks well, then stir about ½ cup of the hot milk mixture into them. Stir the yolk mixture back into the saucepan. Return the saucepan to medium heat and, stirring the filling constantly, bring it to a boil, then cook it for 1 minute.

To avoid a runny filling, this additional minute of cooking is important. If it's not done, amylase, an enzyme in the egg yolk, will react with the starch in the flour and thin out the filling.

Remove the filling from the heat, and stir in the butter and the vanilla, then ½ cup of the coconut.

Pour the warm filling into the piecrust, and allow it to cool while you make your meringue.

Preheat your oven to 350°F.

Using a clean whisk, whisk the egg whites with the remaining ⅛ teaspoon of salt until the mixture is stiff. Gradually beat in the remaining 6 tablespoons of sugar until the mixture is glossy, and the sugar is dissolved. To determine whether the sugar is dissolved, rub a bit of the meringue between your fingers. If it feels gritty, beat it for a minute longer, then test it again.

Spread the meringue evenly over the pie filling, and seal it to the crust. Sprinkle the meringue with the remaining ¼ cup of coconut. Place the pie in the oven, and bake it for 20 minutes, or until the meringue is delicately browned.

Banana Cream Pie

Bananas made their first appearance in America in 1870, when sea captain Lorenzo Baker brought a load from Jamaica to New Jersey. They were a featured as a luxury item at the 1876 Philadelphia Centennial Exposition, but improved transportation soon made them affordable.

1   prebaked piecrust (see page 18)
3   large eggs
¾   cup plus 6 tablespoons granulated sugar, divided
½   cup unbleached all-purpose flour
¼   teaspoon plus ⅛ teaspoon salt, divided
2½ cups whole milk
1   tablespoon salted butter
1   teaspoon vanilla extract
2   firm medium bananas, or 3 small

Separate the eggs, placing the yolks in a 2-cup glass measure, and the whites in a large mixing bowl.

In a large saucepan, combine ¾ cup of the sugar, the flour, and ¼ teaspoon of the salt.

In a separate pan, scald the milk, and then pour it over the dry ingredients, stirring them constantly until everything is well mixed. Place the large saucepan over medium heat, and cook the milk mixture, stirring it constantly, until it is smooth and thick, about 2 minutes. Remove it from the heat.

Whisk the egg yolks well, then stir about ½ cup of the hot milk mixture into them. Stir the yolk mixture back into the saucepan. Return the saucepan to medium heat and, stirring the filling constantly, bring it to a boil, then cook it for 1 minute.

To avoid a runny filling, this additional minute of cooking is important. If it's not done, amylase, an enzyme in the egg yolk, will react with the starch in the flour and thin out the filling.

Remove the filling from the heat, and stir in the butter and the vanilla. Slice the bananas about ¼ inch thick, and add them to the filling.

Pour the warm filling into the piecrust, and allow it to cool while you make your meringue.

Preheat your oven to 350°F.

Using a clean whisk, whisk the egg whites with the remaining ⅛ teaspoon of salt until the mixture is stiff. Gradually beat in the remaining 6 tablespoons of sugar until the mixture is glossy, and the sugar is dissolved. To determine whether the sugar is dissolved, rub a bit of the meringue between your fingers. If it feels gritty, beat it for a minute longer, then test it again.

Spread the meringue evenly over the pie filling, and seal it to the crust. Place the pie in the oven, and bake it for 20 minutes, or until the meringue is delicately browned.

Cherry Cream Pie

This is an old variation on cream pie that is rarely seen anymore. If you use cherries from a can or jar, rather than fresh or frozen, skip the instructions for cooking them; just drain them really well and reserve ¼ cup of the liquid.

1	prebaked piecrust (see page 18)
1	pound fresh sour cherries, 2 cups frozen, or 1 cup canned
¼	cup water
¾	cup plus 8 tablespoons granulated sugar, divided
3	large eggs
½	cup unbleached all-purpose flour
¼	teaspoon plus ⅛ teaspoon salt, divided
2¼	cups whole milk
1	tablespoon salted butter

If you're using fresh cherries, measure out 2 cups, and pit them. Sour cherries are simple to pit by hand: squeeze the cherry gently and the stone pops out the stem end.

Place the fresh cherries, or unthawed frozen ones, in a medium saucepan. Add the water and 2 tablespoons of the sugar. Over medium heat, cook the cherries, uncovered, stirring them occasionally, until they are tender, about 4 minutes. Drain them well, reserving ¼ cup of the liquid.

Separate the eggs, placing the yolks in a 2-cup glass measure, and the whites in a large mixing bowl.

In a large saucepan, combine ¾ cup of the sugar, the flour, and ¼ teaspoon of the salt.

In a separate pan, scald the milk, and then pour it over the dry ingredients, stirring them constantly until everything is well mixed. Place the large saucepan over medium heat, and cook the milk mixture, stirring it constantly, until it is smooth and thick, about 2 minutes. Remove it from the heat.

Whisk the egg yolks well, then whisk the reserved cherry liquid into them. Stir about ½ cup of the hot milk mixture into the yolk mixture. Stir the yolk mixture back into the saucepan. Return the saucepan to medium heat and, stirring the filling constantly, bring it to a boil, then cook it for 1 minute.

To avoid a runny filling, this additional minute of cooking is important. If it's not done, amylase, an enzyme in the egg yolk, will react with the starch in the flour and thin out the filling.

Remove the filling from the heat, and stir in the butter, then fold in the cherries.

Pour the warm filling into the piecrust, and allow it to cool while you make your meringue.

Preheat your oven to 350°F.

Using a clean whisk, whisk the egg whites with the remaining ⅛ teaspoon of salt until the mixture is stiff. Gradually beat in the remaining 8 tablespoons of sugar until the mixture is glossy, and the sugar is dissolved. To determine whether the sugar is dissolved, rub a bit of the meringue between your fingers. If it feels gritty, beat it for a minute longer, then test it again.

Spread the meringue evenly over the pie filling, and seal it to the crust. Place the pie in the oven, and bake it for 20 minutes, or until the meringue is delicately browned.

Lemon Meringue Pie

Oranges, lemons, and limes came from the Caribbean colonies and were generally found only on the tables of the very wealthy. The Quakers receive credit for inventing lemon custard in the late 1700s, and it is a testament to their frugality, as it required only one lemon to create an entire dish. Philadelphia pastry chef Elizabeth Goodfellow took lemon custard and turned it into a pie in the early 1800s.

  1   prebaked piecrust (see page 18)
  3   large eggs
  1   large lemon, or ⅓ cup lemon juice
  ¾   cup plus 6 tablespoons granulated sugar, divided
  ⅓   cup unbleached all-purpose flour
  ⅓   cup cold water
  1   cup boiling water
  1   tablespoon salted butter
  ⅛   teaspoon salt

Separate the eggs, placing the yolks in a 2-cup glass measure, and the whites in a large mixing bowl.

Juice the lemon, measuring out ⅓ cup.

In a large saucepan, combine ¾ cup of the sugar, the flour, and the cold water. Stirring the mixture constantly, gradually add the boiling water. Place the saucepan over medium heat, and cook the mixture, continuing to stir it, until it is thick, about 2 minutes. Remove the saucepan from the heat.

Whisk the egg yolks well, then whisk the lemon juice into them. Stir about ½ cup of the hot mixture into the yolk mixture, then stir it back into the saucepan. Return the saucepan to medium heat and, stirring the filling constantly, bring it to a boil, then cook it for 1 minute. Remove the filling from the heat, and stir in the butter.

To avoid a runny filling, the additional minute of cooking is important. If it's not done, amylase, an enzyme in the egg yolk, will react with the starch in the flour and thin out the filling.

Pour the warm filling into the piecrust, and allow it to cool while you make your meringue.

Preheat your oven to 350°F.

Using a clean whisk, whisk the egg whites with the remaining ⅛ teaspoon of salt until the mixture is stiff. Gradually beat in the remaining 6 tablespoons of sugar until the mixture is glossy and the sugar is dissolved. To determine whether the sugar is dissolved, rub a bit of the meringue between your fingers. If it feels gritty, beat it for a minute longer, then test it again.

Spread the meringue evenly over the pie filling, and seal it to the crust. Place the pie in the oven, and bake it for 20 minutes, or until the meringue is delicately browned.

CHAPTER SIX

Fruit (Sort of) Pies

These first recipes are in the order of the harvest, from rhubarb in the spring to apples and grapes in autumn. The last five recipes are winter, or year-round, pies. Although most fruit pies can be topped with either a solid crust or a latticed one, some do require a solid crust in order to cook properly. To avoid having a fruit pie with a runny filling, bake it the full amount of time, then let it cool completely before cutting it. (This last thing can be very hard to do.)

Rhubarb Pie

You'll find rhubarb (which is technically a vegetable) referred to as "pie plant" in old recipe books.

1	double piecrust
1½	pounds rhubarb (about 10 medium stalks)
¾	cup granulated sugar
2	tablespoons unbleached all-purpose flour
2	tablespoons salted butter

Preheat your oven to 350°F.

Trim the ends off the rhubarb stalks, and cut them into ½-inch pieces. Measure out 4 cups.

In a large bowl, mix the sugar and the flour. Add the rhubarb and toss it until it is well coated.

Pile the rhubarb mixture in the piecrust so it is slightly mounded in the middle.

You may top this pie with either a solid crust, or a woven lattice.

For a solid crust, place the top crust over the filling, and with your fingers or the tines of a fork, crimp the edges of the pie well. With a sharp knife, cut vents in the top crust.

For a lattice crust, cut ¾-inch-wide strips of crust, weave over the filling, and with your fingers or the tines of a fork, crimp the edges of the pie well.

Place the pie in the oven, and bake it until the filling is thick and bubbly, about 1 hour 15 minutes.

Strawberry Rhubarb Pie

Strawberries were coming into season as rhubarb went out, so this was a natural combination. The sweet strawberries complement the tart rhubarb beautifully.

1	double piecrust
¾	pound strawberries (about 24 medium)
¾	pound rhubarb (about 5 medium stalks)
½	cup granulated sugar
3	tablespoons unbleached all-purpose flour
2	tablespoons salted butter

Preheat your oven to 350°F.

Hull the strawberries, and cut them in half. Measure out 2 cups.

Trim the ends off the rhubarb stalks, and cut them into ½-inch pieces. Measure out 2 cups.

In a large bowl, mix the sugar and the flour. Add the strawberries and rhubarb and toss them until they are well coated.

Pile the fruit mixture in the piecrust so it is slightly mounded in the middle.

You may top this pie with either a solid crust, or a woven lattice.

For a solid crust, place the top crust over the filling, and with your fingers or the tines of a fork, crimp the edges of the pie well. With a sharp knife, cut vents in the top crust.

For a lattice crust, cut ¾-inch-wide strips of crust, weave over the filling, and with your fingers or the tines of a fork, crimp the edges of the pie well.

Place the pie in the oven, and bake it until the filling is thick and bubbly, about 1 hour 15 minutes.

Cherry Pie

Sweet cherries were for eating, but sour cherries were for pies. (The old name for the sour cherry tree was "pie cherry tree.") Sour cherries have a very brief season, from late June to early July. Montmorency is the most common variety available today, although North Stars or English Morellos can sometimes be found. About pitting cherries: I don't own a cherry pitter because a young woman picking cherries for her family showed me a very simple method of doing it by hand—squeeze the cherry gently and the stone pops out the stem end.

1 double piecrust
2 pounds sour cherries
¾ cup granulated sugar
3 tablespoons unbleached all-purpose flour
2 tablespoons salted butter

Preheat your oven to 350°F.

Pit the cherries, and measure out 4 cups.

In a large bowl, mix the sugar and the flour. Drain the cherries of any accumulated juices, add them to the sugar mixture, and toss everything well.

Pile the cherry mixture in the piecrust so it is slightly mounded in the middle.

You may top this pie with either a solid crust, or a woven lattice.

For a solid crust, place the top crust over the filling, and with your fingers or the tines of a fork, crimp the edges of the pie well. With a sharp knife, cut vents in the top crust.

For a lattice crust, cut ¾-inch-wide strips of crust, weave over the filling, and with your fingers or the tines of a fork, crimp the edges of the pie well.

Place the pie in the oven, and bake it until the filling is thick and bubbly, about 1 hour 15 minutes.

Blackberry Pie

The traditional name for blackberry was "bramble," so in some old recipe books you'll find this called bramble pie.

  1 double piecrust
  ½ cup granulated sugar
  3 tablespoons unbleached all-purpose flour
  4 cups blackberries
  2 tablespoons salted butter

Preheat your oven to 350°F.

In a large bowl, mix the sugar and the flour. Add the blackberries and gently combine everything.

Pile the blackberry mixture in the piecrust so it is slightly mounded in the middle, and dot the top with the butter.

You may top this pie with either a solid crust, or a woven lattice.

For a solid crust, place the top crust over the filling, and with your fingers or the tines of a fork, crimp the edges of the pie well. With a sharp knife, cut vents in the top crust.

For a lattice crust, cut ¾-inch-wide strips of crust, weave over the filling, and with your fingers or the tines of a fork, crimp the edges of the pie well.

Place the pie in the oven, and bake it until the filling is thick and bubbly, about 1 hour 15 minutes.

Raspberry Pie

Most of the raspberries that come to market nowadays are red, but black, purple, and even golden varieties can be found from time to time. Red raspberries tend to be the tartest; if you're making your pie with one of the others, you may want to reduce the sugar by a quarter cup.

1	double piecrust
¾	cup granulated sugar
3	tablespoons unbleached all-purpose flour
4	cups raspberries
2	tablespoons salted butter

Preheat your oven to 350°F.

In a large bowl, mix the sugar and the flour. Add the raspberries and gently combine everything.

Pile the raspberry mixture in the piecrust so it is slightly mounded in the middle, and dot the top with the butter.

You may top this pie with either a solid crust, or a woven lattice.

For a solid crust, place the top crust over the filling, and with your fingers or the tines of a fork, crimp the edges of the pie well. With a sharp knife, cut vents in the top crust.

For a lattice crust, cut ¾-inch-wide strips of crust, weave over the filling, and with your fingers or the tines of a fork, crimp the edges of the pie well.

Place the pie in the oven, and bake it until the filling is thick and bubbly, about 1 hour 15 minutes.

Blueberry Pie

Blueberry pie. This was the one that almost did me in, trying to find the balance between sweet and tart, with a filling that was firm but not gelatinous, and the fruit still intact.

- 1 double piecrust
- ½ cup granulated sugar
- 3 tablespoons unbleached all-purpose flour
- 4 cups blueberries
- 2 tablespoons salted butter

Preheat your oven to 350°F.

In a large bowl, mix the sugar and the flour. Add the blueberries and gently combine everything.

Pile the blueberry mixture in the piecrust so it is slightly mounded in the middle, and dot the top with the butter.

You may top this pie with either a solid crust, or a woven lattice.

For a solid crust, place the top crust over the filling, and with your fingers or the tines of a fork, crimp the edges of the pie well. With a sharp knife, cut vents in the top crust.

For a lattice crust, cut ¾-inch-wide strips of crust, weave over the filling, and with your fingers or the tines of a fork, crimp the edges of the pie well.

Place the pie in the oven, and bake it until the filling is thick and bubbly, about 1 hour 15 minutes.

Huckleberry Pie

Huckleberries grow in the high mountains of Montana. They are often confused with blueberries, which have a very similar taste. Huckleberries have bigger seeds and a thicker skin, and the flavor is a little more tart and intense.

1	double piecrust
¼	cup plus 2 tablespoons granulated sugar
3	tablespoons unbleached all-purpose flour
4	cups huckleberries
2	tablespoons salted butter

Preheat your oven to 350°F.

In a large bowl, mix the sugar and the flour. Add the huckleberries and gently combine everything.

Pile the huckleberry mixture in the piecrust so it is slightly mounded in the middle, and dot the top with the butter.

You may top this pie with either a solid crust, or a woven lattice.

For a solid crust, place the top crust over the filling, and with your fingers or the tines of a fork, crimp the edges of the pie well. With a sharp knife, cut vents in the top crust.

For a lattice crust, cut ¾-inch-wide strips of crust, weave over the filling, and with your fingers or the tines of a fork, crimp the edges of the pie well.

Place the pie in the oven, and bake it until the filling is thick and bubbly, about 1 hour 15 minutes.

Gooseberry Pie

Gooseberries and fresh currants are from the same family. To make currant pie, simply substitute fresh currants, red, black, or white, for the gooseberries. If you use black or white currants, decrease the sugar by 2 tablespoons, as they are less astringent than the other fruits.

1	double piecrust
¾	cup granulated sugar
3	tablespoons unbleached all-purpose flour
4	cups gooseberries
2	tablespoons salted butter

Preheat your oven to 350°F.

In a large bowl, mix the sugar and the flour. Add the gooseberries and gently combine everything.

Pile the gooseberry mixture in the piecrust so it is slightly mounded in the middle, and dot the top with the butter.

You may top this pie with either a solid crust, or a woven lattice.

For a solid crust, place the top crust over the filling, and with your fingers or the tines of a fork, crimp the edges of the pie well. With a sharp knife, cut vents in the top crust.

For a lattice crust, cut ¾-inch-wide strips of crust, weave over the filling, and with your fingers or the tines of a fork, crimp the edges of the pie well.

Place the pie in the oven, and bake it until the filling is thick and bubbly, about 1 hour 15 minutes. The filling may seem liquid when you remove the pie from the oven, but it will set up as it cools.

Peach Pie

The "old folks" I've spoken with swear by cling peaches for their taste and texture.

1   double piecrust
2   pounds peaches (about 8 medium or 12 small)
½   cup granulated sugar
3   tablespoons unbleached all-purpose flour
2   tablespoons salted butter

Preheat your oven to 350°F.

Pare the peaches, and slice them ¼ inch thick, to make 4 cups.

In a large bowl, mix the sugar and the flour. Add the peaches and gently combine everything.

Pile the peach mixture in the piecrust so it is slightly mounded in the middle, and dot the top with the butter.

You may top this pie with either a solid crust, or a woven lattice.

For a solid crust, place the top crust over the filling, and with your fingers or the tines of a fork, crimp the edges of the pie well. With a sharp knife, cut vents in the top crust.

For a lattice crust, cut ¾-inch-wide strips of crust, weave over the filling, and with your fingers or the tines of a fork, crimp the edges of the pie well.

Place the pie in the oven, and bake it until the filling is thick and bubbly, about 1 hour 15 minutes.

Crab Apple Pie

Crab apples are the only apple native to North America. They look rather like a cherry-size apple, and are in season briefly in August.

1   double piecrust
2   pounds crab apples
1   cup granulated sugar
2   tablespoons unbleached all-purpose flour
2   tablespoons salted butter

Preheat your oven to 350°F.

Quarter, but don't pare, the crab apples, and scoop out the seeds. Measure out 4 cups of fruit.

In a large bowl, mix the sugar and the flour. Add the crab apples and gently combine everything.

Pile the crab apple mixture in the piecrust so it is slightly mounded in the middle, and dot the top with the butter.

Place the top crust over the filling, and with your fingers or the tines of a fork, crimp the edges of the pie well. With a sharp knife, cut vents in the top crust.

Place the pie in the oven, and bake it until the filling is thick and bubbly, about 1 hour.

Apple Pie

Use a variety of apple that is firm and tart. I like Wolf River for an early apple, and Northern Spie later in the season. I've listened to a number of heated discussions about the best pie apple, but many old-timers in New England swear by Rhode Island Greenings.

1   double piecrust
2   pounds apples (about 4 medium-large)
½   cup granulated sugar
1   tablespoon unbleached all-purpose flour
2   tablespoons salted butter

Preheat your oven to 350°F.

Core and pare the apples, then slice them ¼ inch thick. Measure out 4 cups.

In a large bowl, mix the sugar and the flour. Add the apples and gently combine everything.

Pile the apple mixture in the piecrust so it is slightly mounded in the middle, and dot the top with the butter.

You may top this pie with either a solid crust, or a woven lattice.

For a solid crust, place the top crust over the filling, and with your fingers or the tines of a fork, crimp the edges of the pie well. With a sharp knife, cut vents in the top crust.

For a lattice crust, cut ¾-inch-wide strips of crust, weave over the filling, and with your fingers or the tines of a fork, crimp the edges of the pie well.

Place the pie in the oven, and bake it until the filling is thick and bubbly, about 1 hour.

Pork Apple Pie

Old-time New Englanders used salt pork from soup to dessert. This pie, which was a favorite of President Calvin Coolidge, was often served for the Sunday evening meal.

1 double piecrust
2 ounces fat salt pork
2 pounds apples (about 4 medium-large)
½ cup granulated sugar
1 tablespoon unbleached all-purpose flour
½ teaspoon ground cinnamon
¼ teaspoon ground nutmeg

Preheat your oven to 350°F.

Dice the salt pork into pea-size pieces.

Core and pare the apples, then slice them ¼ inch thick. Measure out 4 cups.

In a large bowl, mix the sugar, the flour, and the spices. Add the apples and gently combine everything.

Pile the apple mixture in the piecrust so it is slightly mounded in the middle, and dot the top with the salt pork.

Place the top crust over the filling, and with your fingers or the tines of a fork, crimp the edges of the pie well. With a sharp knife, cut vents in the top crust.

Place the pie in the oven, and bake it until the filling is thick and bubbly, about 1 hour.

Grape Pie

This pie originated in the German communities that lined the eastern shore of Lake Erie. Concord grapes are traditionally used, but any tart, slip-skin grape would do.

1	double piecrust
2½	pounds Concord grapes
½	cup granulated sugar
3	tablespoons unbleached all-purpose flour
2	tablespoons salted butter

Preheat your oven to 350°F.

Stem the grapes and measure out 4 cups. Using your thumb and forefinger, slip the skins from the grapes and allow the pulp to fall into a 2-quart saucepan. Reserve the skins in a large bowl. Bring the pulp to a boil, remove it from the heat, and put it through a sieve or a colander to remove the seeds. Let it cool.

Add the pulp, the sugar, and the flour to the reserved skins.

Pour the grape mixture in the piecrust, and dot the top with the butter.

You may top this pie with either a solid crust, or a woven lattice.

For a solid crust, place the top crust over the filling, and with your fingers or the tines of a fork, crimp the edges of the pie well. With a sharp knife, cut vents in the top crust.

For a lattice crust, cut ¾-inch-wide strips of crust, weave over the filling, and with your fingers or the tines of a fork, crimp the edges of the pie well.

Place the pie in the oven, and bake it until the filling is thick and bubbly, about 1 hour.

Shaker Lemon Pie

In the early part of the 19th century, citrus fruits were very expensive, so the Shakers, being simple and frugal, wanted to use the whole lemon. The longer the lemons macerate, the softer the rind becomes.

- 3 medium lemons
- 2 cups granulated sugar
- 1 double piecrust
- 4 large eggs

Slice the lemons very thin, as thinly as you can, leaving the rind on, and remove the seeds. In a medium bowl, combine the lemon slices and the sugar. Let the mixture stand at least 24 hours, stirring it occasionally.

Preheat your oven to 350°F.

In a small bowl, whisk the eggs until they are light in color, then add them to the lemons, and stir. Pour the filling into the piecrust.

Place the top crust over the filling, and with your fingers or the tines of a fork, crimp the edges of the pie well. With a sharp knife, cut vents in the top crust.

Place the pie in the oven, and bake it until the filling puffs up the crust, about 45 minutes.

Raisin Pie

This was also called Funeral Pie. Because it could be made at any season of the year, and kept well when prepared a day or two ahead, it was often served with the meal following a funeral.

- 1 double piecrust
- 2 cups raisins
- 2 cups water
- ½ cup granulated sugar
- ¼ cup unbleached all-purpose flour
- 2 tablespoons salted butter

Preheat your oven to 350°F.

In a medium saucepan, combine the raisins and the water. Bring the water to a boil over medium heat, then lower the heat and simmer the raisins, uncovered, for 5 minutes, or until the raisins are plump. Remove the saucepan from the heat.

In a medium bowl, mix the sugar and the flour. Slowly stir in ½ cup of the hot liquid from the raisins. When the mixture is smooth, stir it back into the saucepan.

Return the saucepan to low heat. Stirring constantly, bring the mixture to a full simmer and cook it until it is thickened, about 3 minutes. Remove the filling from the heat, and stir in the butter.

Allow the raisin mixture to cool to room temperature, then pour it into the piecrust.

Place the top crust over the filling, and with your fingers or the tines of a fork, crimp the edges of the pie well.

Place the pie in the oven, and bake it for 50 minutes, or until the filling is thick and bubbly.

Sour Cream Raisin Pie

Although I was never able to determine the origins of this pie, I've found it on menus across the heartland of America; this recipe came to me by way of Kansas. Traditionally, sour cream was referred to as soured cream, and came about naturally when bacteria caused fresh cream to sour. Modern sour cream is made using a carefully controlled process of fermentation.

1	double piecrust
2	cups raisins
2	cups water
¾	cup granulated sugar
¼	cup unbleached all-purpose flour
⅛	teaspoon salt
1	cup sour cream
1	teaspoon ground cinnamon

Preheat your oven to 350°F.

In a medium saucepan, combine the raisins and the water. Bring to a boil over medium heat, then lower the heat and simmer, uncovered, for 5 minutes, or until the raisins are plump. Remove the saucepan from the heat.

In a medium bowl, mix the sugar, the flour, and the salt. Slowly stir in ½ cup of the hot liquid from the raisins. When the mixture is smooth, stir it back into the saucepan.

Return the saucepan to low heat. Stirring constantly, bring the mixture to a simmer and cook until it has thickened, about 3 minutes. Remove the filling from the heat. Stir in the sour cream and cinnamon, then pour the raisin mixture into the piecrust.

Place the top crust over the filling and, with your fingers or the tines of a fork, crimp the edges of the pie well.

Place the pie in the oven, and bake it for 50 minutes, or until the top crust is golden brown.

Mincemeat Pie

Mincemeat, or mince, originated in England as a way to preserve meat. This old recipe comes from Maine. It makes enough for three pies, and will keep indefinitely in the refrigerator. You can also use reconstituted dried mincemeat, which makes a very good pie, or mincemeat from a jar.

1	double piecrust
1	pound lean beef
½	pound beef suet
1	pound apples (about 2 medium-large)
1	pound raisins (about 2 cups)
¼	pound citron
1	quart apple cider
2	cups granulated sugar
½	pound dried currants, or 1 cup
1	teaspoon ground cinnamon
1	teaspoon ground mace
½	teaspoon salt
¼	teaspoon ground cloves
¼	teaspoon ground allspice
¼	teaspoon ground nutmeg
1	cup brandy

Mince the beef, then do the same with the suet.

Pare, core, and finely chop the apples. Coarsely chop the raisins and the citron.

In a stockpot, combine all the ingredients, except the brandy. Bring the mixture to a boil, then lower the heat to low. Cook the mincemeat, uncovered, for 2 hours, stirring it occasionally. Remove the pot from the heat, and let the mincemeat cool. When it is cool, but not cold, stir in the brandy. Pour the mincemeat into glass jars, and refrigerate it for at least

1 week. The old recipe calls for letting the mincemeat stand in a crock for a week before using it, and says that it will keep indefinitely in a cool place.

Measure out 3 cups of the mincemeat, and pour it into the piecrust.

You may top this pie with either a solid crust, or a woven lattice.

For a solid crust, place the top crust over the filling, and with your fingers or the tines of a fork, crimp the edges of the pie well. With a sharp knife, cut vents in the top crust.

For a lattice crust, cut ¾-inch-wide strips of crust, weave over the filling, and with your fingers or the tines of a fork, crimp the edges of the pie well.

Place the pie in the oven, and bake it for 50 minutes, or until the filling is thick and bubbly.

Mock Apple Pie

As pioneers settled the American West, they found themselves without access to apples, which had been a staple food "back East." So some resourceful cooks came up with a substitute pie made from soda crackers. During the American Civil War, apples, coming as they did from New England, became scarce in the South. In 1863, a recipe for "Apple Pie Without the Apples" appeared in the **Confederate Receipt Book:** *"To one small bowl of crackers, that have been soaked until no hard parts remain, add one teaspoonful of tartaric acid, sweeten to your taste, add some butter, and a very little nutmeg."*

1	double piecrust
2	cups sugar
2	teaspoons cream of tartar
1¾	cups water
16	soda crackers or large common crackers
½	teaspoon ground cinnamon
2	tablespoons salted butter

Preheat your oven to 350°F.

In a medium saucepan, mix the sugar and the cream of tartar. Gradually stir in the water. Bring the mixture to a boil over high heat, then lower the heat to low, and allow it to simmer for 10 minutes. Remove the pan from the heat and let the syrup cool for 10 minutes.

Coarsely break the crackers, and measure out 1¾ cups of crumbs.

Spread the crumbs evenly in the piecrust, then pour the sugar syrup over the crumbs. Sprinkle the cinnamon over the filling, then dot the top with the butter.

Place the top crust over the filling, and with your fingers or the tines of a fork, crimp the edges of the pie well.

Place the pie in the oven, and bake it for 30 minutes.

U.S./Metric Measurement Conversions

VOLUME

U.S.	METRIC
1 teaspoon	5 milliliters
1 tablespoon	15 milliliters
¼ cup	59 milliliters
⅓ cup	79 milliliters
½ cup	118 milliliters
¾ cup	177 milliliters
1 cup	237 milliliters
4 cups (1 quart)	.95 liter
4 quarts (1 gallon)	3.8 liters

WEIGHT

U.S.	METRIC
½ ounce	14 grams
1 ounce	28 grams
8 ounces	227 grams
12 ounces	340 grams
16 ounces (1 pound)	454 grams

COMMON BAKING INGREDIENTS

INGREDIENT	U.S.	METRIC
1 cup all-purpose flour	5 ounces	142 grams
1 cup whole wheat flour	5½ ounces	156 grams
1 cup granulated (white) sugar	7 ounces	198 grams
1 cup packed brown sugar (light or dark)	7 ounces	198 grams
1 cup cocoa powder	3 ounces	85 grams

Butter:

	U.S.	METRIC
¼ cup = 4 tablespoons = ½ stick	2 ounces	57 grams
⅓ cup = 5⅓ tablespoons = ⅔ stick	2⅔ ounces	75 grams
½ cup = 8 tablespoons = 1 stick	4 ounces	113 grams
1 cup = 16 tablespoons = 2 sticks	8 ounces	226 grams

COOKING TEMPERATURE

To convert Fahrenheit to Celsius, subtract 32 from the Fahrenheit temperature, then divide the result by 1.8. The 350 degrees Fahrenheit at which all these pies bake would be 177 degrees Celsius.